CHILDREN'S EDUCATIONAL

JUNIOR
LEONARDO DA VINCI

ISBN: 978-1492171058

Cover image: The Mona Lisa, 1503-1507.

Title image: Self-portrait in Red Chalk by Leonardo da Vinci, 1512-1515.

This page: Study for the Head of Leda, 1505-1507.

CONTENTS

Leonardo *da* Vinci means...

Leonardo *of* Vinci.

INTRODUCTION

I am very jealous of the Queen. She owns just one of a few sets of tatty old notebooks. You might wonder what is so special about somebody's old scrawled notes. The answer is that *these* notes were written by an amazing man named Leonardo da Vinci (say: Lee-on-are-doh da Vin-chee).

Leonardo da Vinci was a **genius** (jee-nee-us). Some people are really clever but a genius is someone who is so brilliant that they make all the very clever people look like nothing special. There are plenty of very clever people around in this world but there are only a few geniuses.

One of Leonardo's Notebooks

The fact that Leonardo was a genius at art would be hard to disagree with because he painted the most famous painting in the world today—The Mona Lisa (Mow-na Lee-sa). (She is on the cover of this book). But there are other artists who were also geniuses. The thing that sets Leonardo apart from them is that as well as being a genius artist he was a genius scientist and inventor too! If I'm being honest, he was pretty brilliant at maths, music and making maps as well. He was what we call a **polymath** (pol-ee-math) which is someone who knows lots of different subjects well. 'Poly' means 'many' in Greek.

LEONARDO'S LIFETIME

To understand just how clever Leonardo was we need to look at what life was like at the time he lived. He was born so long ago (over 500 years ago) that it can be hard to grasp the importance of the things he did because today we are so used to them that they don't seem that special.

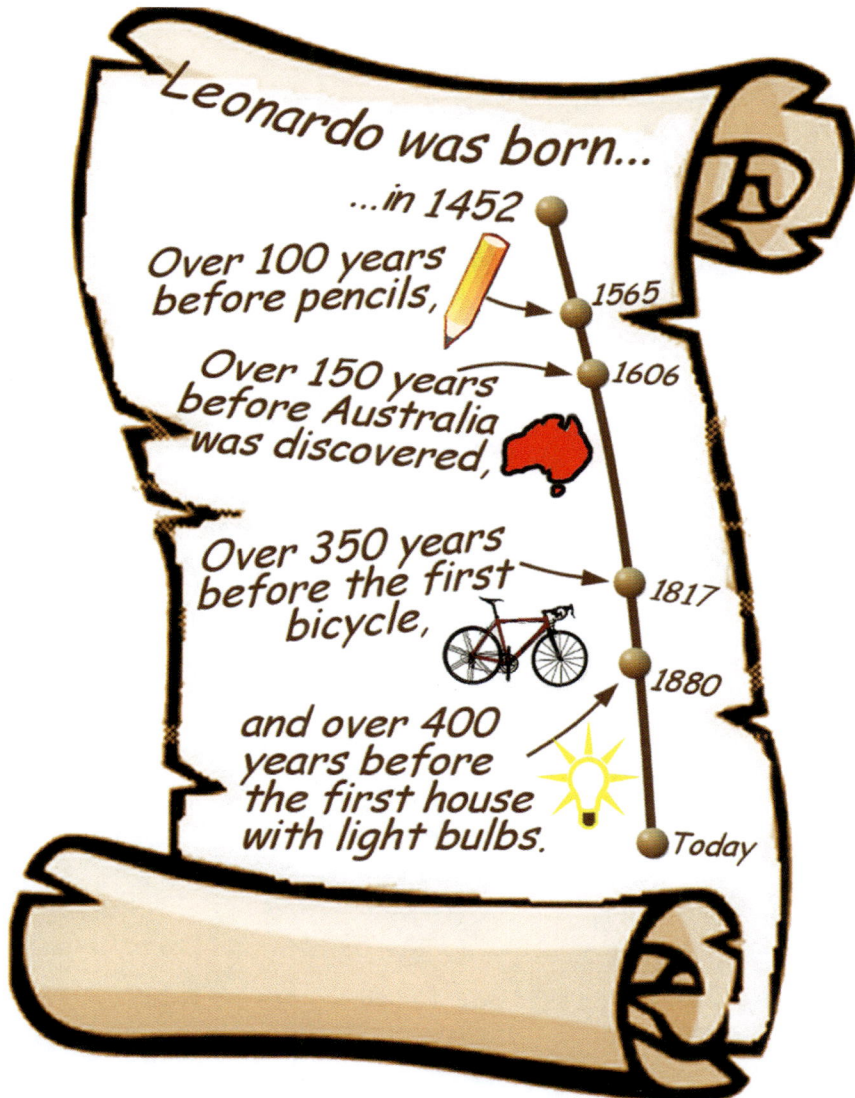

Leonardo was born...

...in 1452

Over 100 years before pencils, → 1565

Over 150 years before Australia was discovered, → 1606

Over 350 years before the first bicycle, → 1817

and over 400 years before the first house with light bulbs. 1880

Today

Rich Cities

The small village of Vinci, where Leonardo was born, is near to a beautiful city called Florence (Flor-en-s). Today Florence is in Italy, which is an easy country to remember because it is shaped like a lady's boot, but back then the country we now know as Italy didn't

Today

North

France

Italy

Greece

Leonardo's Time

France

Ottoman Empire

M
V

F

R

Silk, spices & dyes

R = Rome
M = Milan (Mi-lan)
V = Venice (Ven-iss)
F = Florence (Flor-en-s)

exist. Instead, each of the big cities in that part of the world was more like a separate mini country and each was under the control of a different powerful family.

These cities (or **city states** as we call them) were rich because of where they were. They stood at a gateway between the Ottoman (Ot-oh-man) Empire to the east and the rest of Europe to the north and west. This meant that the people could buy things like silks, spices and dyes from the East and then sell them on at a higher price in Europe.

The powerful families in these city states would often fight over their land and they loved to show off their money. One way to do this was to pay people to make new bigger and better art and inventions than ever before. The families were locked in a battle to make sure that they had **luxuries** (luck-sure-ees) that the other ones couldn't have. A luxury is something we like to have but don't really need.

All this meant that if you were clever you could make a living serving these rich families and that is exactly what Leonardo did. But it was a scary life; some of them were cruel (one ruler killed his own brother and would invite people to dinner and then poison them). Getting such people to pay him was not always easy.

The Rebirth of Learning

There was one good thing that came out of all this plotting. For the 800 years before these families the church had been all-powerful and it had wanted art to follow set rules. It could be colourful but it was to be kept very simple. The job of art was to tell the stories of the bible and nothing more. The church didn't wanted change and so art didn't change much and very few new things were invented. Because of this those 800 years are called 'The Dark Ages'.

Now that these rich families were trying to out-do each other, they started a new wave of thinking. For the first time people were paid to use their **imagination** (im-aj-in-ay-shone). They were rewarded for inventing things and changing the way things were done. People looked everywhere for new ideas and one place they found help was in books that had been written before The Dark Ages, back in the time of the Greeks and the Romans before Jesus was born. In these books they found art, science and maths that had been forgotten. It is for this reason that we call the time that Leonardo lived 'The **Renaissance**' (Ren-ace-on-s) which means 'Rebirth' in Italian.

Mary

Painted in 1308   Painted by Leonardo in 1508

Here are two paintings of Mary and Jesus. Leonardo makes his people look real by painting dark shadows and bright highlights on their skin, just as the Greeks had. The other one, done 200 years earlier, is more like Dark Age art. The people are quite flat, like in old cartoons. Which do you prefer?

Everyday Life

Most people still lived and worked in the countryside outside the cities. They farmed the land using only the most basic machines. Ships were still powered by wind or oars. There were no bikes, no cars and certainly no aeroplanes. The idea of a flying machine would have been thought **ridiculous** (rid-ic-you-lus) (something to laugh at).

There was no electricity or even running water from taps as we have today. If you wanted water you had to go to the well and get it. A machine to print books had just been invented so because most books were still handwritten they were rare. There was no such thing as a newspaper let alone the internet.

If you wanted to learn a skill, like painting, saddle-making or shipbuilding you would go to the workshop of a master craftsman and take up an **apprenticeship** (a-pren-tiss-ship). This meant that you would help the master with his jobs and in return he would teach you. It was to the workshop of a master artist in Florence that Leonardo went to train when he was 14 years old. At first he would have mixed paints and practised drawing and painting from models. Paint did not come out of a tube; it had to be mixed out of coloured powders and egg yolk or oil which stuck the powder together. (I have put a recipe on the back cover so that you can try making it yourself.)

In time Leonardo would have been allowed to paint small parts of the paintings in the workshop. He is said to have painted just the angel kneeling on the left in the next painting called 'The Baptism of Christ'. Do you think that angel has been done by a different person? [**Baptism** (bap-tis-m) is when you become a member of a church].

When the master saw the angel he said it was so good that from then on only Leonardo was to paint the faces in all the workshop's paintings and he himself would never paint again!

Part of The Baptism of Christ, c. 1475

THE MAKING OF A GENIUS

You might think it a bit strange that someone could be brilliant at both art and science. They seem so different. In fact, there is one simple skill that artists and scientists share. That skill is being able to **observe** (ob-serve) (to look at) things very closely. For example, if I asked—what does a cat look like? One answer might be—a cat has four legs, fur, small pointed ears and whiskers, and that would not be wrong. But if I then tried to draw a cat just from what I've been told we would soon see that it is not nearly enough to go on. Have a look at my drawing that follows. It has everything the answer said but it's not right is it? To draw a cat properly you have to *observe* it in detail and Leonardo did just that.

This animal has fur, small pointed ears, four legs and whiskers, but it is clearly not a cat!

Leonardo's drawings of cats. There is one other animal there, can you spot it?

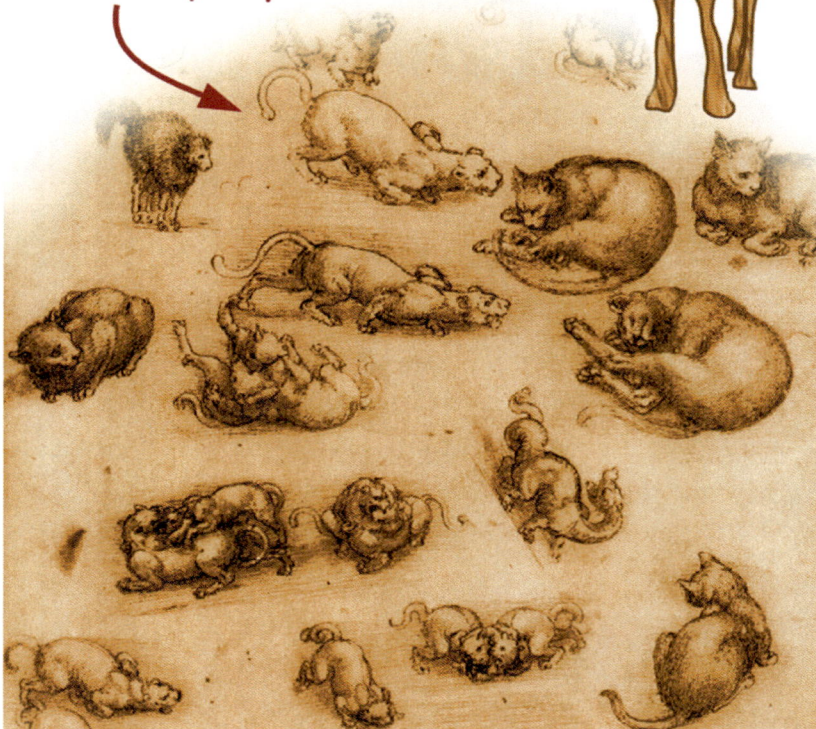

Scientists try to understand how the world around us works. So scientists might be interested in how cats can jump up onto very high walls. To answer this question they would first *observe* cats jumping up walls. Then they would suggest some ideas as to how cats do it and after that they would test those ideas. So the artist and scientist begin at the same starting point—observing things.

Leonardo trained in the workshop for about six years. All that time he worked on his skills. The apprentices would spend hours observing and learning **anatomy** (an-at-omy, the parts of the body). They would have drawn until they knew the tiniest details of the smallest of muscles, like those in your hands. (Have a look at your own hands now and notice all the tiny lumps and bumps on them).

Leonardo also spent hours observing nature: the water ripples on a river, the patterns of wind in a storm, how animals move and more. When you think about it, it's not surprising that he should go on to become a scientist and ask the next natural question—why? Why does the water move like this? How? How do the birds fly?

A Study of Arms and Hands, c. 1474
(c. is short for circa (sir-ka)
meaning 'around about'.)

Leonardo just would not stop trying to answer questions. No answer would do if he had not seen it with his own eyes. It is true that he had grown up when people were re-reading the Greek and Roman books (remember it was called **The Renaissance** (Ren-ace-on-s)) but as a boy he hadn't had proper lessons and he couldn't yet read them very well. This was a good thing because he had to work everything out for himself and the Greeks and Romans had got many things wrong.

Once Leonardo understood how things worked he then took *another* step and used his new knowledge to invent and build things. A person who makes things using their knowledge of science is an **engineer** (en-jin-ear).

The other animal was...

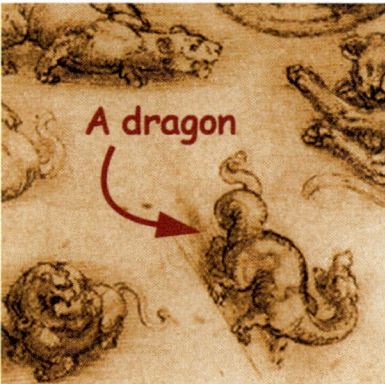

A dragon

But I have said enough about Leonardo's world and the way his mind worked. It's time to take a look at a few of the things he did.

13

INVENTIONS AND DISCOVERIES

Some of Leonardo's inventions wouldn't have worked but many would with only small changes that he would easily have been able to make had they been built. It is possible that he sometimes made mistakes in the drawings on purpose to stop people stealing his ideas.

Flight

Leonardo had a strange habit of buying birds in cages and then setting them free. The people in the markets must have thought he was really odd! He did it because he was **obsessed** (ob-ses-d) with (he could not stop thinking about) how birds fly. He wanted to watch their wings moving over and over again. His notes are full of drawings of birds in flight and they are also full of plans for flying machines. He invented:
– a helicopter (heli-cop-ter),
– a hang-glider,
– a parachute (para-shoot), and even
– a giant set of wings to be strapped on to a man.
His ideas all came from observing nature and the hang-glider and the parachute have been built in modern times and found to work.

Helicopter

Flight

Glider

Parachute

Wings for a man

War Machines

The rich rulers of the city states were always fighting each other. Because of this they didn't just spend their money on luxuries but also on weapons. Leonardo was a peaceful person, he hated the idea of hurting someone, but he had no choice, he had to work. Later in his life he left Florence and travelled to other city states like Milan (Mi-lan) and Venice (Ven-iss) where he designed:

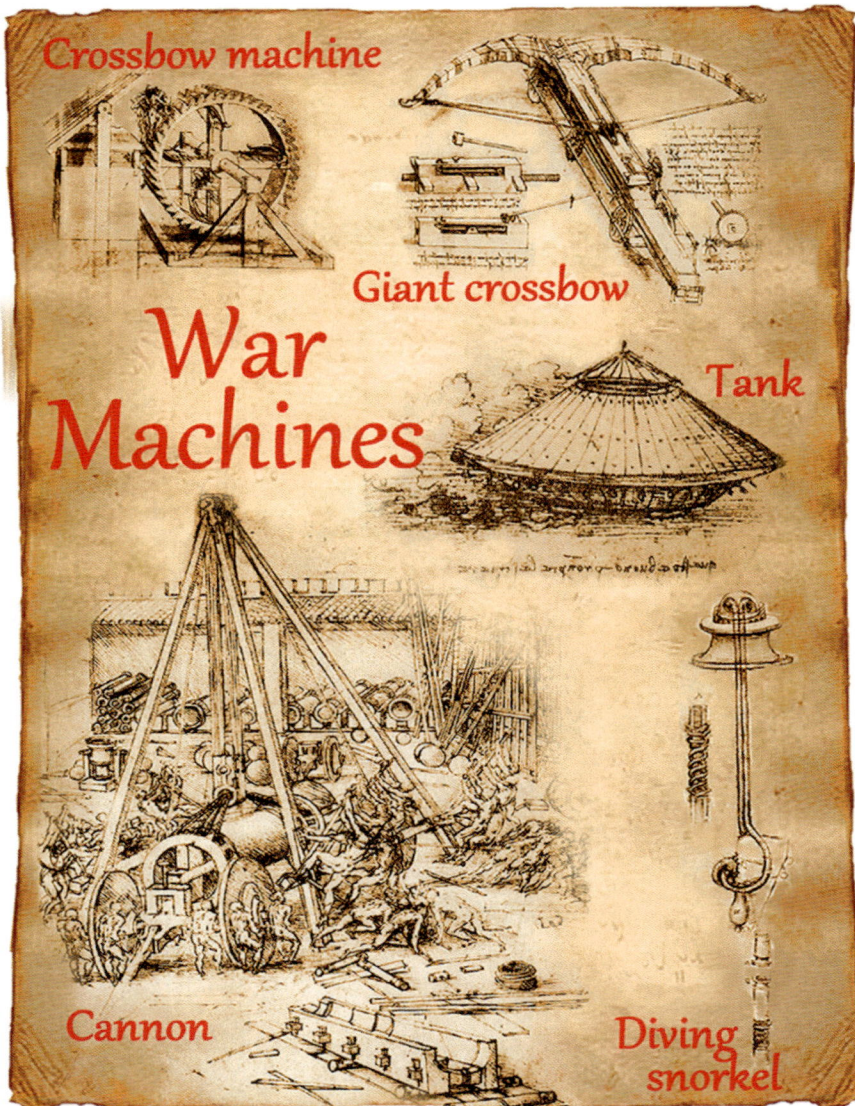

Crossbow machine

Giant crossbow

War Machines

Tank

Cannon

Diving snorkel

– a tank (which looks like a tortoise on wheels) with built in cannons, to protect soldiers as they march on to the battlefield,

– **catapults** (cat-a-pults, machines for throwing heavy stones),

– crossbows,

– bombs with fins to balance them as they fly,

– a bridge that could be packed up and moved, and

– a diving suit with a long snorkel so that the soldiers of Venice could walk along the bottom of the sea to drill holes in enemy ships.

16

Water Machines

He also drew machines powered by water, like watermills and engines, and ways to move water by changing the paths of rivers or sucking it up with a giant pump. To do this he used gearwheels, springs, levers and pulleys and all the tools that engineers use everyday today to lift and move great weights.

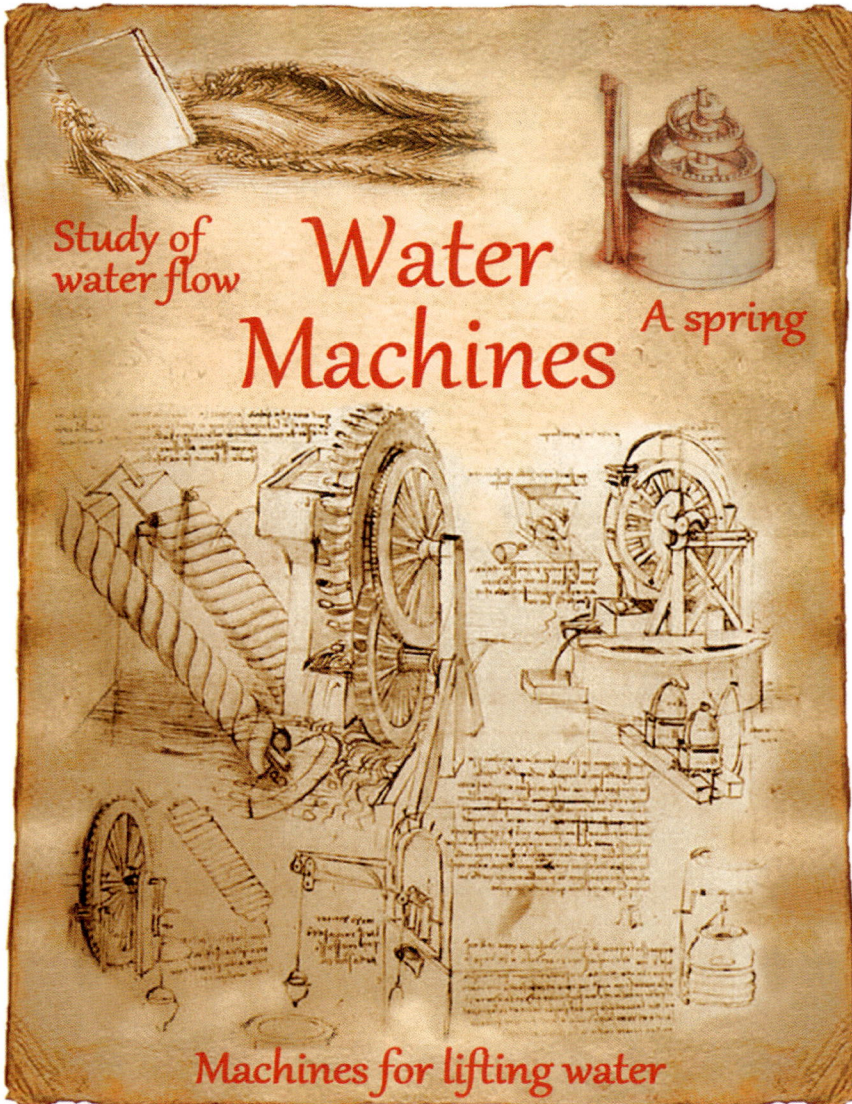

Study of water flow

Water Machines

A spring

Machines for lifting water

The Human Body

As I have already said, all artists learned anatomy (the parts of the body). Leonardo's notes are full of drawings showing the sizes of its different parts. One of his most famous ones is 'Vitruvian (Vit-roo-vee-an) Man'. It can be found nowadays on **Euro** (Your-oh) coins in Italy. The Euro (€) is the money used in many countries in Europe.

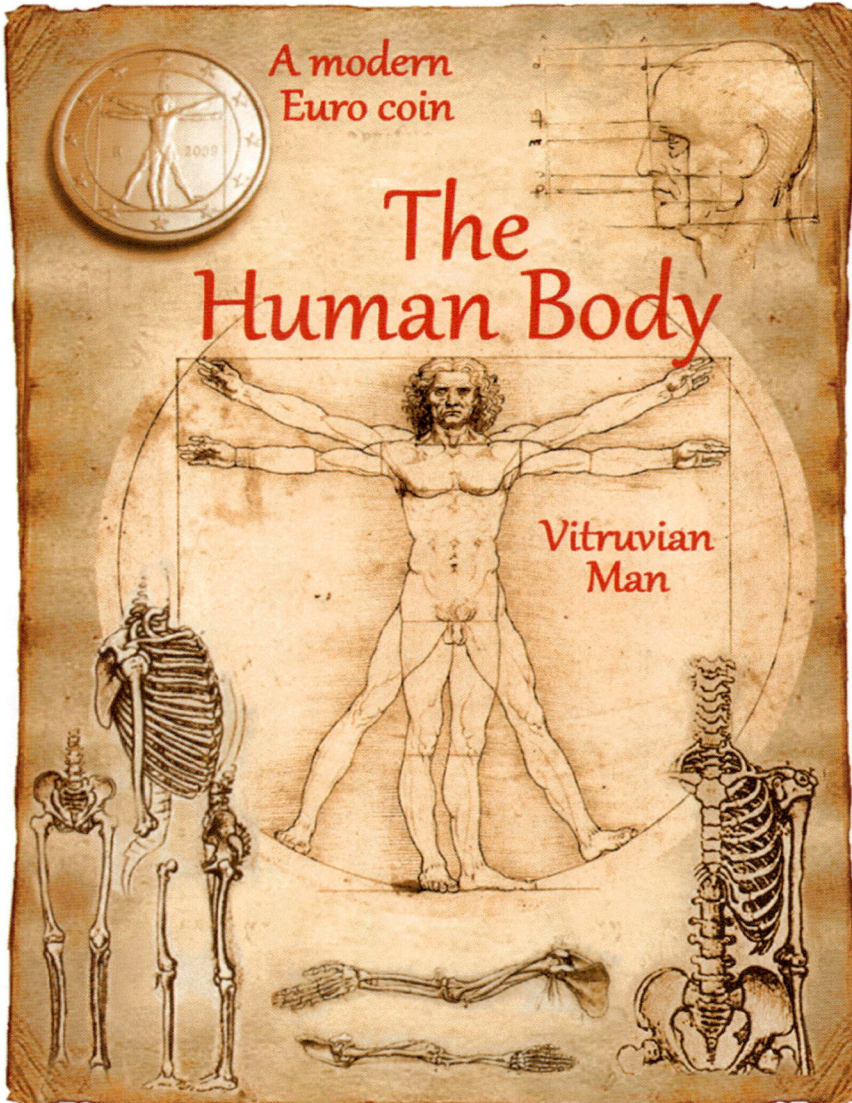

A modern Euro coin

The Human Body

Vitruvian Man

By now you will not be surprised to hear that just knowing the parts of the body was not enough for Leonardo. He wanted to know how they worked. He would often look inside dead bodies to try to find out! This got him into trouble, but he learned some mind-boggling things.

He learned how muscles work to move our bones and he understood it so well that he built a robot which could stand, sit and move its arms. This was a time when people didn't even have tap water and here was a man making a robot! They would never have seen *anything* like it.

He looked at **blood vessels** (the tubes that carry our blood) and saw that an old man's were blocked but those of a young boy were clear. He said that the old man had too much 'food' in his blood. His words may not be those we use today but he wasn't wrong. We now know that if we eat too much fatty food that is exactly what does happen.

Light and the Stars

Since Greek times, people had thought that light came out of our eyes. They thought eyes were like light bulbs in your head! It's easy to spot why this is wrong. Go into a dark room and open your eyes. You don't shine two dots of light on the wall do you? (Not unless you're a Dr Who villain). Leonardo saw that light goes *into* our eyes and that our brains use the pattern created to work out what we're looking at.

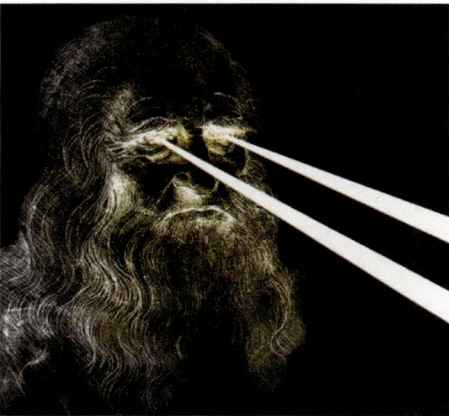

He also spent a lot of time thinking about the light from the stars. He worked out something that is not easy to spot at all. When we wake up in the morning the sun rises in the east. During the day it appears to slowly move through the sky and by the end of the day it sets (goes down) in the west. From the place we are all standing, down on Earth, it looks just as if the sun has done all the moving and we have stayed still. It's not surprising that people thought Earth was the centre of everything and didn't move. They were all wrong and Leonardo amazingly knew it. He knew that the sun does not go around the Earth even though it looks like it does! Today we know that the sun stays still and the Earth **orbits** (or-bits, goes around) it and that it takes the Earth almost exactly one year to orbit the sun.

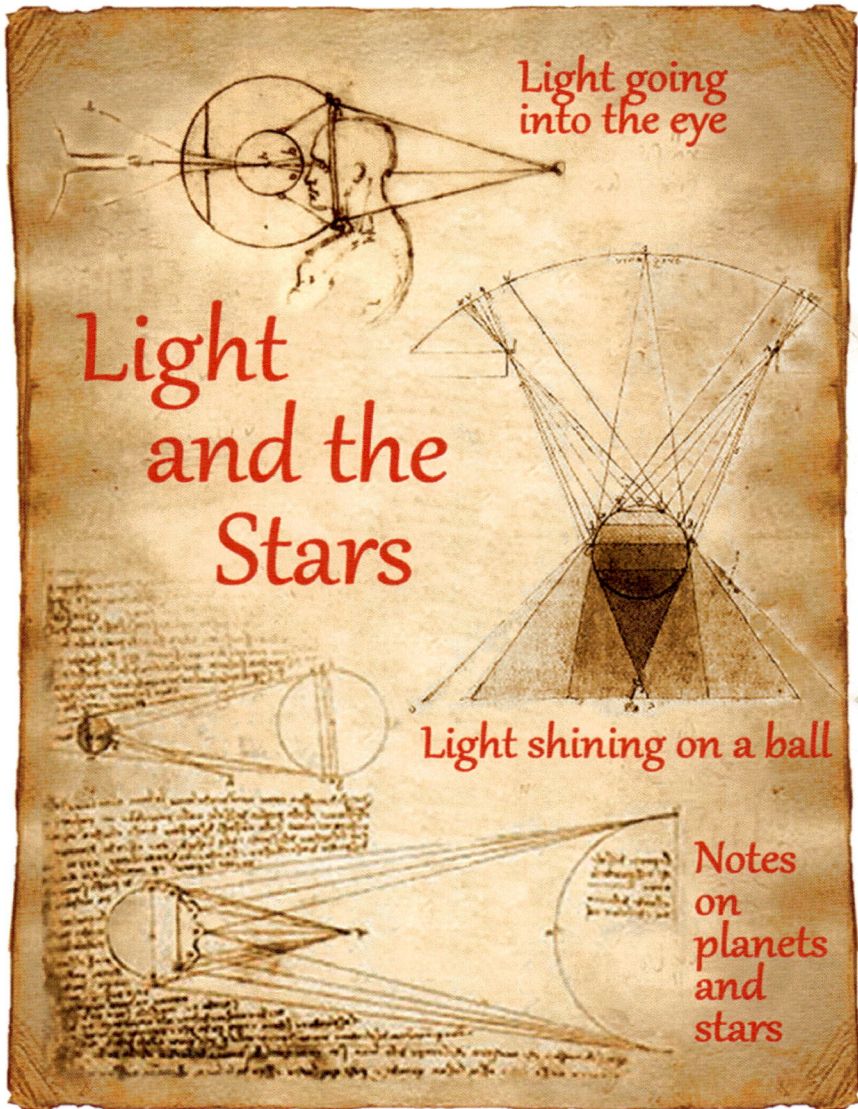

Light going into the eye

Light and the Stars

Light shining on a ball

Notes on planets and stars

SECRET WRITING

Have you noticed something strange about Leonardo's writing? It's hard to spot because it's in Italian. Look up at how he wrote his name. Why does it look odd? Leonardo wrote all his notes in mirror writing. Instead of writing words the normal way round, he wrote their mirror images. To read them you had to look at their reflection in a mirror.

It could be that he did it to keep his notes secret. We do know that he was worried about people stealing his ideas. However, we also know that he was left-handed. By using mirror writing he could write from right to left instead of left to right. This is much easier for a left-handed person. It helps to stop the ink smudging; so it may just have been a practical solution to slow drying ink.

When we put a mirror on the dashed line above, the image revealed is different from the actual writing. The mirror changes what we see. If we place a mirror on a shape and it *doesn't* change what we see, we call the line a line of **symmetry** (sim-it-ree). Here are some shapes with different numbers of lines of symmetry.

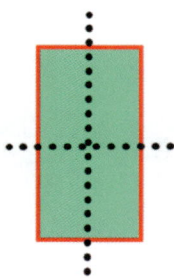

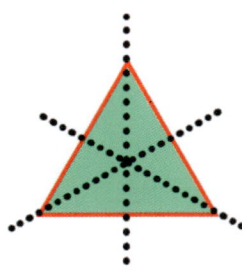

1 line of symmetry

2 lines of symmetry

3 lines of symmetry

NOBODY'S PERFECT

Leonardo may have been a genius but he was far from perfect. He was often so keen to try out a new idea that he would do it at the wrong time. Below is the famous wall painting that he did in the late 1490s for the Duke of Milan. It is of Jesus's 'Last Supper'.

Wall paintings were made by putting wet plaster on a wall and then, straight away, painting into it so that the paint and plaster dried stuck together. You had to rush a bit to finish before the plaster dried.

Leonardo didn't want to rush so he invented a dry plaster to paint on... but he didn't test it first. A few years later it began to crack and peel off. It is still there today but much of it is lost, it is a ghost now compared to what it was.

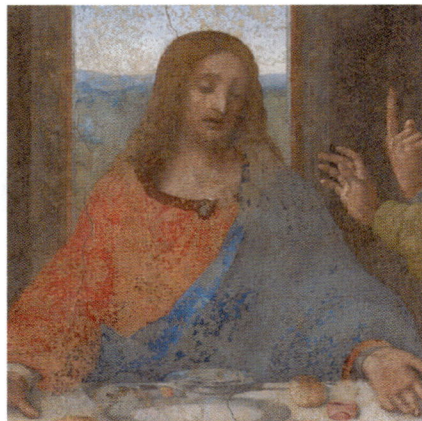

Look at this close-up of just Jesus. You can see how much paint has peeled off.

We learn from our mistakes so we can forgive Leonardo his habit of trying out new things, even if he did sometimes do it at the wrong times. Far worse though was his bad habit of not finishing things. Again and again he would either take years to finish work or even never finish it at all. When he was painting The Last Supper he would work all day one day without stopping, but then not turn up for the next three. Or he would go and stand all day looking at it, paint one brush stroke and then go home! Look back at the painting of Mary and baby Jesus on page 8. Notice that the blue part of Mary's robe has not got its colourful top coat.

It is not surprising that one of the most important painting jobs of that time, to paint the ceiling of a famous chapel in Rome, was not given to Leonardo but to another artist called **Michelangelo** (Mi-kel-an-jel-oh). Michelangelo was trusted to finish it.

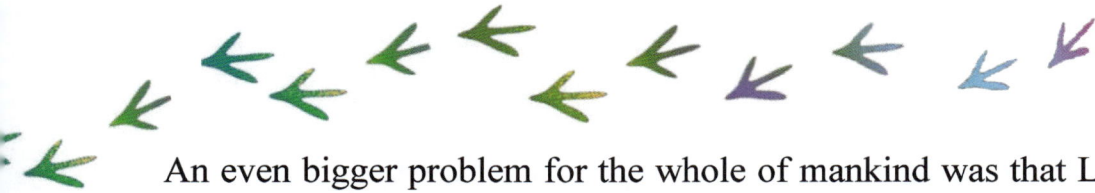

An even bigger problem for the whole of mankind was that Leonardo was the same with his science. When he wanted to understand something he could think of nothing else, but once it was solved it was over. It was gone, dropped, like a young child drops an old toy, and he would move on to the next idea. It's good that he kept notes and that he did revisit some problems but he never tidied his notes up into proper books. They were a mess—13,000 (thirteen thousand) pages all out of order! As a result almost all that discovery was wasted. Nobody used it. It lay lost for hundreds of years and everything that Leonardo had done had to be re-done by later scientists. By the time all the notes we know of were found 400 years later, *everything* had been re-invented.

The ceiling of the Sistine (Sist-een) chapel in Rome. Painted by Michelangelo between 1508 and 1512.

The most famous part is The Creation of Adam (from the story of Adam & Eve). Can you find it in the photos above?

THE MYSTERIES OF THE MONA LISA

The truth is that had it not been for Leonardo's most famous painting, The Mona Lisa, keeping his name known, his notes would probably never have been found at all. But what is so special about her?

At the end of his life Leonardo went to work for King Francis I of France. In Francis he had finally found a friend who understood him. Francis gave him a manor house and it was there that Leonardo died at the age of 67. An imagined scene of his death was painted by the artist **Ingres** (On-gre) 300 years later. The people around Leonardo, including the king, know what a great loss he will be.

The Death of Leonardo da Vinci by Ingres, 1818

When Leonardo died, amongst his things was The Mona Lisa. One of the reasons she is special is that she is *actually* finished. She remains with us as a shining example of all that this great genius had learnt about painting in his long hard life.

She is famous for her slight smile. Because of the special 'smoky' effect Leonardo used, we can never quite work out from it what she is thinking. Unlike other Renaissance paintings she is definitely looking at us as we look at her—something common in portraits today but which Leonardo was, yet again, the first to do. Is she smiling or not? What do you think she is thinking?

The Mona Lisa, 1503-1519

She has other mysteries too. Look closely at the background on the right-hand side. Can you see that the land is higher than on the other side of her head? Also, the water surface on the right-hand side is not flat! It slopes down to the right slightly. After reading this book I need hardly tell you that Leonardo was no fool. He knew that the surface of a lake is always flat so why did he do it like that? Nobody knows. Perhaps he knew how much people love a mystery so he gave us one to keep us talking.

LEARNING FROM LEONARDO

I feel a bit sorry for Leonardo da Vinci. For most of his life he was probably thought of as a bit strange. I'm glad that the people with him at the end of his life understood what a genius he was and what a great loss he would be. In today's world scientists use his methods every day. They base their answers on observation and proof just like he did. But it's easy to do something when everybody else already does it that way. When you're the first person to do it, like Leonardo was, you have to be brave.

We can learn many things from Leonardo. Firstly, **curiosity** (cure-ee-oss-ity) (being interested in knowing things) is not a crime. Be curious and then let your imagination run wild just like he did. Secondly, freethinking (making your own mind up about things) is always the best way. Thirdly, it is healthy to do lots of different things. There is a saying 'the sum is greater than the parts'. Here it means that when you grow up you do not have to *be* one thing, you can *do* many things and you will become a better person for all your different experiences but... the final lesson is to always, *always* finish things. See them right through to the end otherwise all your effort will be wasted. By all means do lots of things but maybe take them just a few at a time.

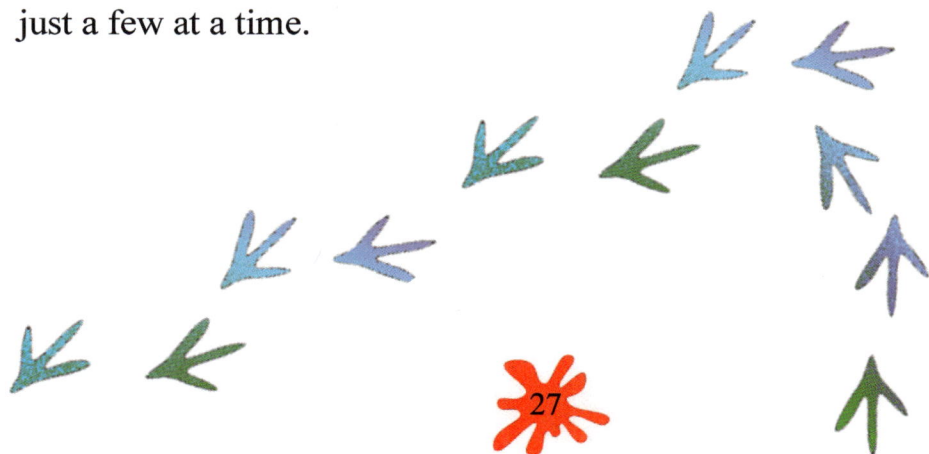

QUIZ

1. What do we call a real person who is very, very clever? a) a genie or b) a genius.

2. Which of these countries was once part of the Ottoman Empire? a) Italy, b) Greece or c) France. [Tip: Have a look at the map on page 6.]

3. What does this mirror writing say? **tloH ɒnoiᖷ**

4. When was The Baptism of Christ painted? a) exactly 1475 or b) around about 1475. [Tip: try looking up the word 'circa' in the glossary.]

5. What does the Greek word 'poly' mean? a) many or b) parrot.

6. What do we mean when we talk about The Dark Ages? a) the time, after the end of the Roman Empire, when very few new things were invented or b) the time before electric light bulbs were invented.

7. How many lines of symmetry do these shapes have?

[Answers follow the glossary.]

a

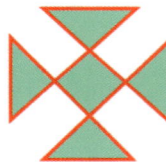
b

c
Tricky question!

28

Glossary

Anatomy (an-at-omy): The parts of the body.

Apprenticeship (a-pren-tiss-ship): A way of learning a new skill by working for a master who is already an expert; in return for your work he teaches you how to do it.

Baptism (bap-tis-m): When you become a member of a church.

Blood vessels: The tubes in animals' bodies that carry their blood.

Catapult (cat-a-pult): A machine for firing stones into the air.

Circa (sir-ka): This is usually shortened to c. You will often see it before a date. It means that we are not sure of it exactly but we know it was around about then.

City state: A city (and its surrounding area) that is ruled as a separate mini country.

Curiosity (cure-ee-oss-ity): Being interested in knowing things.

Engineer (en-jin-ear): A person who builds things using their knowledge of science and maths.

Euro (your-oh): The money used in many parts of Europe.

Genius (jee-nee-us): An extremely clever person.

Ingres (On-gre): A French artist who lived 300 years after Leonardo. He is famous for painting portraits and scenes from history.

Infinite (in-fin-it): An amount that we cannot measure because it would go on forever.

Imagination (im-aj-in-ay-shone): If you use your imagination you are using your mind to picture new ideas for things that do not already exist or have not ever been seen before.

Luxuries (luck-sure-ees): Something we have or want but we don't really need.

Michelangelo (Mi-kel-an-jel-oh): Another artist who lived at about the same time as Leonardo and who is famous for painting the ceiling of the Sistine chapel in Rome.

Observe (ob-serve): To look at.

Obsessed (ob-ses-d): If you are obsessed with something you cannot stop thinking about it.

Orbit (or-bit): To move around in a curved or circular path. Usually used when talking about planets or comets.

Polymath (pol-ee-math): Someone who knows many different subjects well.

Renaissance (Ren-ace-on-s): A rebirth of learning which started in northern Italy in the late 1300s and then spread throughout Europe.

Ridiculous (rid-ic-you-lus): Something silly, to be laughed at.

Symmetry, line of (sim-it-ree): When a mirror is placed along a line of symmetry, the image we see in the mirror is no different from the real shape.

ANSWERS

1. b)
a genius.

2. b)
Greece.

3. It says my name 'Fiona Holt'. Have a go at writing your own name in mirror writing.

St. John the Baptist, 1513-1516
(Believed to be Leonardo's last painting)

4. . b) around about (circa or c.) 1475.

5. a) many.

6. a) the time, after the end of the Roman Empire, when very few new things were invented.

7.

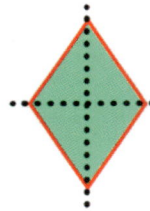
a = 2

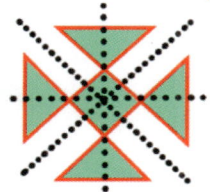
b = 4

7. c) Any line passing through a circle's centre is a line of symmetry so the answer is not a number. The answer is that we cannot count the lines of symmetry. If we kept drawing them with sharper and sharper pencils we would always be able to draw another line between the ones already drawn. It would go on forever. We say the circle has **infinite** (in-fin-it) lines of symmetry.

INDEX OF PICTURES

Want More?

Visit the website and take up the da Vinci design challenge. (Or maybe just colour in some cats.)

ONLINE RESOURCES

To access the online colour slide show which accompanies this book go to **www.theportraitplace.co.uk** and select 'Hardware Solutions' from the 'SMART READS for Kids' dropdown menu.

The login is: **smartcustomer**

The password is: **louvre**

Printed in Great Britain
by Amazon.co.uk, Ltd.,
Marston Gate.